This book shou~
Lancashire County Libr~

Pirate School

Level 4D

Written by Melanie Hamm
Illustrated by Stefano Tamberlini

What is synthetic phonics?

Synthetic phonics teaches children to recognise the sounds of letters and to blend (synthesise) them together to make whole words.

Understanding sound/letter relationships gives children the confidence and ability to read unfamiliar words, without having to rely on memory or guesswork; this helps them to progress towards independent reading.

Did you know? Spoken English uses more than 40 speech sounds. Each sound is called a *phoneme*. Some phonemes relate to a single letter (d-o-g) and others to combinations of letters (sh-ar-p). When a phoneme is written down it is called a *grapheme*. Teaching these sounds, matching them to their written form and sounding out words for reading is the basis of synthetic phonics.

Consultant

I love reading phonics has been created in consultation with language expert Abigail Steel. She has a background in teaching and teacher training and is a respected expert in the field of synthetic phonics. Abigail Steel is a regular contributor to educational publications. Her international education consultancy supports parents and teachers in the promotion of literacy skills.

Reading tips

This book focuses on the ee sound, made with the letter e: ee as in he.

Tricky words in this book

Any words in bold may have unusual spellings or are new and have not yet been introduced.

Tricky words in this book:

recently devious raged agent genius walks

Extra ways to have fun with this book

After the reader has read the story, ask them questions about what they have just read:

Do pirates like sequins?
Which page was your favourite and why?

This is Be Bad Pirate School! You can be bad or clear off!

A pronunciation guide

This grid contains the sounds used in the stories in levels 4, 5 and 6 and a guide on how to say them. /**a**/ represents the sounds made, rather than the letters in a word.

/**ai**/ as in game	/**ai**/ as in play/they	/**ee**/ as in leaf/these	/**ee**/ as in he
/**igh**/ as in kite/light	/**igh**/ as in find/sky	/**oa**/ as in home	/**oa**/ as in snow
/**oa**/ as in cold	/**y+oo**/ as in cube/music/new	long /**oo**/ as in flute/crew/blue	/**oi**/ as in boy
/**er**/ as in bird/hurt	/**or**/ as in snore/oar/door	/**or**/ as in dawn/sauce/walk	/**e**/ as in head
/**e**/ as in said/any	/**ou**/ as in cow	/**u**/ as in touch	/**air**/ as in hare/bear/there
/**eer**/ as in deer/here/cashier	/**t**/ as in tripped/skipped	/**d**/ as in rained	/**j**/ as in gent/gin/gym
/**j**/ as in barge/hedge	/**s**/ as in cent/circus/cyst	/**s**/ as in prince	/**s**/ as in house
/**ch**/ as in itch/catch	/**w**/ as in white	/**h**/ as in who	/**r**/ as in write/rhino

Sounds this story focuses on
are highlighted in the grid.

/**f**/ as in phone	/**f**/ as in rough	/**ul**/ as in pencil/ hospital	/**z**/ as in fries/ cheese/breeze
/**n**/ as in knot/ gnome/engine	/**m**/ as in welcome /thumb/column	/**g**/ as in guitar/ghost	/**zh**/ as in vision/beige
/**k**/ as in chord	/**k**/ as in plaque/ bouquet	/**nk**/ as in uncle	/**ks**/ as in box/books/ ducks/cakes
/**a**/ and /**o**/ as in hat/what	/**e**/ and /**ee**/ as in bed/he	/**i**/ and /**igh**/ as in fin/find	/**o**/ and /**oa**/ as in hot/cold
/**u**/ and short /**oo**/ as in but/put	/**ee**/, /**e**/ and /**ai**/ as in eat/ bread/break	/**igh**/, /**ee**/ and /**e**/ as in tie/field/friend	/**ou**/ and /**oa**/ as in cow/blow
/**ou**/, /**oa**/ and /**oo**/ as in out/ shoulder/could	/**i**/ and /**ai**/ as in money/they	/**c**/ and /**s**/ as in cat/cent	/**y**/, /**igh**/ and /**i**/ as in yes/sky/myth
/**g**/ and /**j**/ as in got/giant	/**ch**/, /**c**/ and /**sh**/ as in chin/ school/chef	/**er**/, /**air**/ and /**eer**/ as in earth/bear/ears	/**u**/, /**ou**/ and /**oa**/ as in plough/dough

Be careful not to add an 'uh' sound to 's', 't', 'p',
'c', 'h', 'r', 'm', 'd', 'g', 'l', 'f' and 'b'. For example,
say 'fff' not 'fuh' and 'sss' not 'suh'.

Behold Captain Ego.

He was feared on all the seven seas. No pirate was his equal.

But **recently** Captain Ego
retired from being a full-time
pirate and established the
Be Bad Pirate School.

He began his first lesson with this
refrain: "If ye wants to be a pirate,
Be a demon of the sea.
Devious, revolting,
That's how we pirates be!"

"Tell me how pirates behave!"
Captain Ego demanded.
"Pirates send emails," said Peter.
"No!" hollered Captain Ego.
"Pirates detest emails."

"Pirates keep lemurs," said Leon.
"No!" shouted Captain Ego.
"Pirates keep parrots."

"Pirates relax in the evening,"
said Eli.
"No!" screamed Captain Ego.
"Pirates never relax."

"Pirates are frequently vegan,"
said Felix.
"No!" bellowed Captain Ego.
"Pirates eat everything."

"Pirates dress in
sequins," said Evie.
"No!" **raged** Captain Ego.
"Pirates find sequins repellent.

Repeat after me:
If ye wants to be a pirate,
Be a demon of the sea.
Devious, revolting,
That's how we pirates be!"

"But I don't want to be a pirate," said Leon. "I want to be a secret **agent**."

"And I want to be a superhero,"
said Peter.

"And I want to be a **genius**," says Eli.

"An evil genius?" says Captain Ego, bewildered.

"No, I want to study meteors," says Eli.

Captain Ego felt betrayed.

"This is Be Bad Pirate School!
You rethinks quick – or you
walks the plank!"
"We will not rethink!" said
the class...

But it was fun to behave like pirates after all!

OVER 48 TITLES IN SIX LEVELS
Abigail Steel recommends...

Other titles to enjoy from Level 4

I love reading phonics — **The Maze** — 978-1-84898-559-9

I love reading phonics — **Fairy Fay's Bad Day** — 978-1-84898-560-5

I love reading phonics — **Eve the Knight** — 978-1-84898-565-0

Some titles from Level 5

I love reading phonics — **Snapped by Sam** — 978-1-84898-561-2

I love reading phonics — **Max's Trip** — 978-1-84898-562-9

I love reading phonics — **George the Genius Gerbil** — 978-1-84898-567-4

Some titles from Level 6

I love reading phonics — **What Wally Wanted** — 978-1-84898-563-6

I love reading phonics — **Superhero Ed** — 978-1-84898-564-3

I love reading phonics — **The Robot Bop** — 978-1-84898-570-4

An Hachette UK Company
www.hachette.co.uk

Copyright © Octopus Publishing Group Ltd 2012
First published in Great Britain in 2012 by TickTock, an imprint of Octopus Publishing Group Ltd,
Endeavour House, 189 Shaftesbury Avenue, London WC2H 8JY.
www.octopusbooks.co.uk

ISBN 978 1 84898 566 7
Printed and bound in China
10 9 8 7 6 5 4 3 2 1